A Gift For:

Sis

From:

Sis
2015

Copyright © 2014 Hallmark Licensing, LLC

Published by Hallmark Gift Books,
a division of Hallmark Cards, Inc.,
Kansas City, MO 64141
Visit us on the Web at Hallmark.com.

All rights reserved. No part of this publication may be reproduced,
transmitted, or stored in any form or by any means without the
prior written permission of the publisher.

Editorial Director: Carrie Bolin
Editor: Emily Osborn
Art Director: Jan Mastin
Designer: Brian Pilachowski
Production Designer: Dan Horton

ISBN: 978-1-59530-844-3
BOK2176

Printed and bound in China
SEP14

Lean on Me

Together We Can Get Through Anything

— BY Ellen Brenneman —

I'm just here to hold up a mirror
so you can see who you really are:
strong, capable,

Brighter, sunnier days
will come.
Easier, happier days
will come.
But a day without me
on your side?

NEVER.

Six things to entertain instead of doubts or regrets:

hope

possibilities

imaginings

dreams

ideas

friendship

Let's take this leap together. That way, wherever we end up,

we may not have a road map,
    but we'll each have a friend.

hat doesn't question, judge,
or set conditions
The kind that just gives
you what you need.

Times like these aren't for sissies.

Good thing you aren't ONe.

You deserve a friend
to share the journey,
to listen, and to care,
even if that friend doesn't always
know the way through.
We don't have to walk
any path alone.

Go out there and conquer
some ice cream.

Every victory
has to start somewhere.

If you've lost your way,
I will be that person
to help you find
your way back there.

With each new day,
I hope you see less of
the shadow
and more of
the sun.

Did you ever see a baby robin take that first leap out of the nest and not figure out how to fly?

Me neither.

If all the world's a stage,
then somebody's got the quill pen
and the ink bottle.

Might as well be you.

Nothing refreshes
the spirit and renews hope
like time...
every day that goes by
brings a bright new sunrise
and twenty-four hours
to dream and plan.

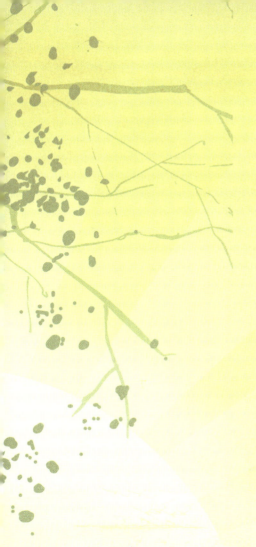

Detours still get you there.

I'm riding shotgun,
 not to backseat drive,
but to help you negotiate
 any tricky twists and turns.
And to insist we stop
 at many coffee shops
  along the way.

Feel free to share it with me.

You don't need me
to tell you to keep going,
keep hoping,
keep believing.
But I will anyway...
because we're friends.

Sisters

If it will help,
I'd rather sit next to you
without saying a word
than get rave reviews
for my standup act.

When this journey's over,
and things are right again,
you'll be well-equipped
to help others with what
you've learned and the strengths
you've gained.

I can look ahead for both of us.
Ahead to the far horizon
where hope leads.

We don't always have to talk

bout deep things.
We can just sit quietly,
letting time take its course—
after all,
time is the best healer.

Resilience means rising above, getting creative, and coming out stronger.

I know you can do it.

Running on empty?

I'll help you
top off your tank.

on the benches all the time
and never be up at bat?
Together, we'll knock
this thing out of the park.

Anything that thinks it can get the best of you clearly doesn't know who it's messing with.

Our kind of friendship
is strong enough
to weather any storm
and resilient enough
to come back stronger
after it's over.

Remember,
where there is a shadow,
there is also
a light shining nearby.

There is no problem that
two friends \ Sisters
cannot ignore, discuss,
plot against, make fun of,
or drown in chocolate sauce.

Our footprints tell us where we've been,

not where we're going.

Sometimes I might not know what to say, but I hope that in my silence, you can hear the caring from deep in my heart.

We have hope,
and we're not afraid
to use it.

We may not be in the same boat, but I'll be your first mate. Let's batten down the hatches and take whichever way will get us to shore.

If you have enjoyed this book
or it has touched your life in some way,
we would love to hear from you.

Please send your comments to:
Hallmark Book Feedback
P.O. Box 419034
Mail Drop 100
Kansas City, MO 64141

Or e-mail us at:
booknotes@hallmark.com